Making Room for His Presence

21-Day Community Devotional

Bobby and Wanda Alger

Partnership
Publications

Partnership Publications
www.h2hp.com

Cover photo by Nathan Mullet

Making Room for His Presence
21-Day Community Devotional
by Bobby and Wanda Alger

© 2015 Bobby and Wanda Alger
Updated 2020

Published by
Partnership Publications
A Division of House To House Publications
11 Toll Gate Road, Litiz, PA, USA
Tele: 717.627.1996

www.h2hp.com

ISBN-10: 0996292438
ISBN-13: 978-0-9962924-3-6

CONTENTS

THE VISION AND PURPOSE OF THIS COMMUNITY DEVOTIONAL

If we are to pursue the manifest presence and power of God in our communities and see the needed cultural shifts in our cities, we must prepare ourselves corporately as the Church. It always starts with personal repentance. But, then these principles must be applied corporately. We need to assess our collective condition and clear out anything that might be hindering the Spirit's work as a community of faith. As we do this, our covenant relationship with Him and with each other is strengthened and the way is prepared for a greater measure of His tangible presence in our midst.

This devotional guide is formatted to use both as individual households and as a corporate Body. It is also recommended to do some kind of fast during this 21-Day experience. Whether it is fasting from food, social media, or some other time-consuming habit, the purpose is to sacrifice something in our lives that will open up more time in His presence.

Though this devotional can be used by just one congregation at a time, the ultimate goal is for several churches within a community to go through this together. It will take more than one congregation or leader to bring the city together and relationships between fellowships need to be nurtured if we are to have any corporate authority in our cities.

We encourage participants to go through the devotional as individual families in the morning and then to meet together as the corporate church every evening for prayer. This will be a sacrifice for most, and yet it will be a tangible way to seek the Lord together and light a fire on the corporate altar of prayer. It is a reminder that we were created to fulfill our mandate together and that our corporate agreement has great power in the spirit.

It is through our confessions of repentance, declarations of truth, and acts of obedience that we become "... a chosen people, a royal priesthood, a holy nation, God's special possession, that (we) may declare the praises of Him who called (us) out of darkness into His wonderful light" (1 Peter 2:9).

DEVOTIONAL FORMAT

The devotional guide is divided into three sections, one for each week:
- Humility versus Pride (Days 1-7)
- Holiness versus Idolatry (Days 8-14)
- Unity versus Division (Days 15-21)

Each daily reading invites the participant to consider action points on a personal level first. It's from the place of personal consecration and passion for His presence that we can pursue God's presence on behalf of our church and community.

But, even as repentance is the starting place to spiritual awakening, we must go beyond merely confessing our sins. Our goal is to experience a divine exchange—our human nature for the divine nature of Christ. We need to be continually filled to overflowing with the power of the Spirit if we are to fulfill our call. We want to become carriers of His presence in our church and in our community.

The Lord declares in Isaiah 66:1, "Heaven is my throne, and the earth is my footstool. Where is the house you will build for me? Where will my resting place be?" We are praying that our communities will be a resting place for the presence of God! As we spend time together in His presence, He will teach us how to become a people of His presence—a place where He can dwell. It is from this place that lasting transformation can happen.

EVENING GATHERINGS

Community breakthrough requires community pursuit. Although our private devotional practices will produce a measure of fruit at home, it's only when we come together as the local body of believers that we will walk into the unity needed for community impact. It is recommended to come together each evening to share in a time of worship, waiting, and repentance before the Lord. As we gather for this purpose, we learn to get comfortable in His presence and listen for corporate directives without distraction.

"Call to me and I will answer you and will tell you great and hidden things that you have not known." (Jeremiah 33:3)

Suggested Format of gatherings

- Corporate worship (Two songs of preparation)
- Devotional Reading for the Day
- Listening and waiting on the Lord (10-15 minutes)
- Personal confessions at the cross (10-15 minutes)
- Corporate prayer in small groups (10-15 minutes)
- Closing Benediction

  To maintain a good level of participation, it is recommended to not go longer than 1 ½ hours every evening.

Practical tips for Facilitation

Leadership: Although a core of leaders will be giving oversight during this fast, it is recommended to include leaders in the evening gathering from a variety of congregations, ministries, businesses, etc. The goal is to honor one another and demonstrate a fuller expression from within the city-wide Church. (The best places to use other leaders are in giving a welcome, reading the devotional and leading the benediction).

Worship: A smaller team is recommended in order to remove any undue focus on platform ministry. The purpose of the worship is to prepare our hearts for waiting on the Lord, not for showcasing a team.

Time of Waiting and Reflection: During this time, it is recommended to play some pre-recorded instrumental music that will allow the congregation to wait and listen. (Worship songs with words can be distracting to some. The goal is to listen for HIS voice and not the voices of others.)

Personal Confessions: Following the time of waiting, open up a time of repentance. These are confessions to the Lord (not to one another). Have a microphone facing a cross on or near the stage for easy access. A leader can read the Action Points and then invite participants to the cross as the Spirit directs them (music can continue softly in the background).

- Keep confessions short and in first person by using "I" not "we."
- If someone is confessing something at the mic that others bear witness to, they are encouraged to stand in their place in agreement. This allows for more people to participate during this time. This is a powerful way

to take both an individual and corporate stand for righteousness as we get our hearts right with the Lord and with one another.

Corporate Prayers: Following the time of personal confessions, small groups can be formed (mix with others not from your own congregation!) Prayers can continue using Corporate Action Points or other themes the Lord may highlight.

- Take pleasure in hosting these gatherings by creating an atmosphere of warmth, safety and intimacy in worship. Make it easy for people to enter in!

WHY REPENTANCE?

"If my people, who are called by my name, will humble themselves and pray and seek my face and turn from their wicked ways, then will I hear from heaven and will forgive their sin and will heal their land."
(2 Chronicles 7:14)

Repentance is more than merely confessing our sins. It is turning away from our fleshly responses and choosing to live and walk in the power of the Spirit. The transformation we seek will only come about through a people of God's presence who have turned away from sin and are actively demonstrating the heart of God through their life and conduct. Repentance is not the goal, but the starting point from which the Holy Spirit can come and heal, deliver, and restore. When we have done our part, God can do His. His manifest presence can complete the task as we position ourselves for Him to come.

WEEK ONE
HUMILITY VERSUS PRIDE

Day 1: Humility Defined

Day 2: Living Low

Day 3: Succeeding With Grace

Day 4: The Joy of Correction

Day 5: Letting Holy Spirit Do His Job

Day 6: Comparisons Prohibited

Day 7: Who Am I?

DAY 1: HUMILITY DEFINED

"And what does the LORD require of you; but to do justice, to love kindness, and to walk humbly with your God" (Micah 6:8).

Humility is not so much defined in the Bible as it is demonstrated by the One who is humble. Humility is a central character trait of God as seen through Jesus Christ. The Old Testament word translated humility means "gentleness" and "helper." The New Testament word for humility means "lowly in mind or position." Humility is serving others as unto the Lord.

Pride is self-focused and self-absorbed. It presumes to know, better than God, how to follow His Word. We can fall into this trap by thinking we can find a different way and still achieve the same results on our own. Human beings are born with the root of pride in their lives. Jesus, however, was born with the root of humility in his life. Becoming born again removes the root (nature) of pride and plants within us the root (nature) of humility. Renewing the mind is a must in order to conquer pride's residue and embrace the full benefits of humility.

Jesus rarely told people who He was, but rather served them, taught them, and showed them God's love. He veiled his title to promote His Father! Humble people have surrendered their wills to God regardless of cost. Humble people will not explain away God's Word when it goes contrary to personal convenience. Humble people will not listen to the voice of man, over the voice of God's word.

PERSONAL ACTION POINTS
- Is title important to you?
- Is being recognized flattering—or not being recognized shattering?
- Do you serve others regardless of acknowledgement or praise?
- Confess any self-interest and ask the Lord for a clean heart and pure motives.

CORPORATE ACTION POINTS
- Confess any need for recognition as a ministry or congregation.
- Confess any fear of man you may be harboring.
- Ask for a greater fear of the Lord.
- Pray for a greater desire to serve than to be served.

DAY 2: LIVING LOW

"Elisha sent a messenger to him, "Go, wash yourself seven times in the Jordan, and your flesh will be restored and you will be cleansed." But Naaman went away angry and said, "I thought that he would surely come out to me and stand and call on the name of the Lord his God, wave his hand over the spot and cure me of my leprosy"
(2 Kings 5:10).

How many times have we inwardly wished for God to come and promote us through some public event? When it does not happen, we may outwardly get enraged or inwardly become defeated.

The world instructs us to get promoted through education, information, and being friends with the right people. Jesus promotes us through our willing obedience to be "seen by God rather than man." Promotion from God comes through private time spent with God (Matthew 6:5-6). Jesus taught the humble will inherit the earth (Matthew 5:5) which means go "low and slow" not "fast and furious" as the world says.

Jesus taught that humility is the prerequisite for honor. Increased grace is given to the humble (or afflicted), but the proud are resisted by God. The Lord rescues the humble regardless if they are righteous kings (2 Chronicles 32:24-26), wicked leaders (2 Chronicles 33:12-13) or common folk (2 Chronicles 30:8-11). Humility is not a personality trait, but a CHOICE to live low in regards to position, title, or academic achievement. Even if we have the abilities, talents or gifts to propel us forward, we wait on God's timing until He promotes or approves us.

PERSONAL ACTION POINTS
- Do you have any anger towards God for not promoting you in some way?
- Have you been secretly hoping that public recognition would propel you into the spotlight?
- Repent and ask the Lord to bring you into his plan for promotion!

CORPORATE ACTION POINTS
- Repent of any desire to be seen and noticed by others in the community.
- Confess preoccupation with honor.
- Choose to live humbly in service to other ministries and congregations.

DAY 3: SUCCEEDING WITH GRACE

"God opposes the proud but gives grace to the humble." Submit your-selves, then, to God. Resist the devil, and he will flee from you. Come near to God and he will come near to you" (James 4:7, 8).

We are most familiar with the need for humility as it relates to being a sinner. Some people suggest that we deliberately sin to stay humble. Others encourage Christians to live under self-condemnation in order to remain humble. Both suggestions are a great misunderstanding of God's truth! The fact is sin does not humble us, grace does! The grace that forgives and sets us free is very humbling!

Humility is what brings us the grace to be obedient and fulfill our purpose. Jesus exemplified joyful humility: "Who for the joy set before him endured the cross, scorning its shame" (Hebrews 12:2-3). Jesus took joy in submitting to his Father's will and serving others while He was on earth. Biblical humility is more than a deep sorrow in repentance. It is the joy of following through with what God has spoken. God's grace is what makes it possible to succeed in our call (Titus 2:11-14).

Humility is the heart soil in which grace can grow! Humility is making a choice to come near to God, so He will come near to us with His grace. When we walk in this humility, His grace will become evident and our walk will be much easier and succeed. Grace-filled humility makes the enemy flee!

PERSONAL ACTION POINTS
- Is there any area of your life that does not exhibit humility with grace?
- Is anything standing between you and God as you draw near to Him?
- Forgive those who impose a religious view of humility and those who do not model grace-filled humility explained in God's Word.

CORPORATE ACTION POINTS
- Repent for preaching a gospel of works instead of grace.
- Ask the Holy Spirit to pour out a revelation of God's grace to overcome shame or guilt.
- Pray for leaders to walk in the joy-filled grace that demonstrates the humility of Christ.

DAY 4: THE JOY OF CORRECTION

"My son, do not despise the LORD's discipline and do not resent his rebuke, because the LORD disciplines those he loves, as a father the son he delights in" (Proverbs 3:11-12).

Nobody likes to be told they're wrong! However, for most Christians, it's not always due to outright arrogance or pride. Sometimes, it's fear of failure. We have such high expectations for ourselves that we begin to despair if we don't meet our own standard. But, when you look at it, that attitude is another form of pride! Perfectionism is a form of pride because it focuses on our performance rather than God's grace.

If a father or mother truly loves their children, they will correct them. It's not punishment, however; it's training for the future. We discipline our children so they learn how to become godly sons and daughters in God's kingdom. The goal is not only to correct behavior but also to train their hearts. This is what God does with us. He is forming our hearts and character to think, feel, see and hear like He does. If we start going off track, He will lovingly correct us to get us realigned to His heart.

We don't only need God's correction but also each other's. The Church talks a lot about accountability, but few know what it really means. Biblical accountability is not telling someone they should be accountable or telling them what's wrong. It's inviting someone into your life to hold you accountable for what God is teaching you. This takes great grace and great humility, yet it is the very thing that forms Christ-like character.

PERSONAL ACTION POINTS
- Do you resent being corrected?
- Do you fear failure?
- Repent of these attitudes and of pride or perfectionism.
- Ask God to renew your mind to see discipline as a good thing!

CORPORATE ACTION POINTS
- Repent of rebellion towards spiritual authority.
- Ask the Holy Spirit to cleanse the Church from ungodly authority.
- Ask forgiveness for not listening to the Lord's correction for the Church.
- Pray for leaders to be healed so they can lead from a place of wholeness.

DAY 5: LETTING HOLY SPIRIT DO HIS JOB

"Why do you look at the speck of sawdust in your brother's eye and pay no attention to the plank in your own eye?" (Matthew 7:3).

When we see weaknesses or failures in others, we must humble ourselves and let God have His way. We have not been given the right to change anyone nor do we have any ability to save them. The job to convict and to save is God's alone.

Jesus did not condemn sinners. He condemned hypocrites. A hypocrite is a "play actor"—one who excuses his own sin while pointing out the sin of others. Without a focus of humility we would all become hypocrites, unable to see our two-faced life. Hypocrites can't see flaws within themselves but focus on the flaws in others. Hypocrites have no mercy because they are operating under God's judgment. Ultimately, no hypocrite will find holiness without first being humbled. Humility is one of the first steps towards transformation.

At some point in our lives, we will face the impurities in our hearts. We will respond in two ways: become a hypocrite or become humbled. The Holy Spirit's job within us it to make us holy after the likeness of Jesus Christ. In his book, *4 Keys to Hearing God's Voice*, Dr. Mark Virkler says that positive thoughts come from the Holy Spirit, negative/condemning thoughts come from the devil, and analyzing thoughts come from within ourselves. The Holy Spirit's job is not to condemn us but to deepen our love and knowledge of the grace offered in Jesus. Humility is the starting point for that journey.

PERSONAL ACTION POINTS
- Are you quick to criticize others before examining your own heart?
- In what ways might you be hypocritical?
- Ask the Lord to give you a heart of compassion for those with whom you don't agree.

CORPORATE ACTION POINTS
- Repent of the need to correct others.
- Repent of hypocrisy in the Church.
- Pray for each church in the city to hear the Father's voice of love and grace, not judgment.

DAY 6: COMPARISONS PROHIBITED

"... but when they measure themselves by themselves and compare themselves with themselves, they are without understanding. It is not he who commends himself that is approved, but he whom the Lord commends" (2 Corinthians 10:12, 18 NASU).

One of the easiest sins to succumb inadvertently to when we are pursuing God is to keep score and compare ourselves to others. Often we compare not only our supposed successes but also our perceived failures. Even with a sincere desire to grow in the Lord, we can fall prey to the temptation either to be prideful of our revelations or condemned by our weaknesses.

Generally people unintentionally slip into the comparison mindset when feeling insecure. If we are not grounded in our identity in Christ, we look for ways to "add up" and feel accepted. The Word says that when we operate in comparisons, we are without understanding. Other versions say "not wise" and one version even says we're "foolish" when we compare! This is not God's way to spiritual health!

God's way is to first thank Him for those who exhibit Christ-like qualities that we want to emulate. We can be encouraged and strengthened by these attributes without comparing. Second, we should refuse to feel shame or guilt if we don't appear to be "as good" as someone else. If we try to validate ourselves, we'll fall flat. God rewards and commends those who are faithful to Him. When we are tempted to compare ourselves to others, remember Jesus' words to Peter when he asked about John's journey: "What is that to you? You follow Me" (John 21:22).

PERSONAL ACTION POINTS
- Confess ways in which you have compared yourself with others.
- Ask the Lord to reveal any insecurity in your life or need for validation.
- Allow the Holy Spirit to affirm who you are in Christ.

CORPORATE ACTION POINTS
- Repent of comparisons within the Church.
- Confess ways in which the Church has been competitive.
- Ask Holy Spirit to release the heart of Jesus to build others up and commend the strengths and gifts of other ministries.

DAY 7: WHO AM I?

"Now Moses was a very humble man, more humble than anyone else on the face of the earth" (Numbers 12:3).

Why is this statement made about Moses? He certainly didn't start out being humble. Instead Moses started out by using his own strength in trying to rescue God's people. Moses left Egypt humiliated and defeated. After Moses spent forty years in the desert, God sent him back to Egypt with a whole different motivation—walking in humility (Acts 7:20-32). At first, Moses only saw his weaknesses. He asked God, "Who am I? What do I say? What if they will not listen to me? I can't speak well in public!" (Exodus 3:1-4:13).

How did Moses make the change from humiliated to humble? God said, "With him I speak face to face, clearly and not in riddles; he sees the form of the LORD." Moses' identity got settled when he got settled in God. When Moses spoke with God face to face in clear understandable terms, self-preoccupation and false humility were broken off. Humility takes our eyes off our inabilities and puts them on God's abilities. We are no longer bound by ourselves but free in Him.

When humility has taken root in your life, then you will say, "I am not the great I AM, but by the grace of God, I am what I am" (1 Corinthians 15:10). Getting in God's presence puts things into perspective and secures our identity in Him apart from the seeming limitations of self.

PERSONAL ACTION POINTS
• Are you focused on your weaknesses and inabilities more than God's strength and His abilities?
• Repent of all self-preoccupation.
• Declare your trust in God's ability to accomplish His work in you.

CORPORATE ACTION POINTS
• Are we overly preoccupied with the shortcomings in our family, workplace or congregation?
• Have we settled our identity in who we are and what our purpose is?
• Ask the Lord to show you where He is working in these areas.
• Choose to embrace the identity and purpose He's given for your family, your work and your church.

WEEK TWO
HOLINESS versus IDOLATRY

DAY 8: HOLINESS DEFINED

"Therefore come out from them and be separate, says The Lord"
(2 Corinthians 6:17).

The words "holy" and "sanctified" are often interpreted to mean righteous or pure or something similar. But the basic concept of the Hebrew word "qadosh" and its variations is that of apartness and distinction. The true biblical understanding of holiness is to be set apart for God's purposes.

Holy does not mean divine, it doesn't mean good and it isn't gained by following the rules. The concept of being holy or sanctified is not a question of being morally or ethically good; it means you are dedicated to Someone. This is a daily choice in how you live and think. It isn't so much about what you do, but it's whose you are.

Just as a bride sets herself apart for her husband, keeping him as the love of her life and center of her affections, so we are called to be set apart for Christ, alone. We do not keep the Ten Commandments because we should but because we want to out of our love relationship with Jesus. That's why we are to *be holy*—not *do holy*.

The challenge is our willingness to be different than the world. It's not popular to be set apart for God. There are those who will not understand and will mock the things we hold dear. Yet, we have a Lover and Lord who is worth that price. Will you be set apart for Him?

PERSONAL ACTION POINTS
- Rededicate yourself to the Lord—soul, spirit, mind and body.
- Confess any tendency to simply follow the rules instead of considering how your thoughts and actions affect the Lover of your soul.

CORPORATE ACTION POINTS
- Pray for more wholehearted love and devotion in corporate worship as a reflection of our love relationship with Jesus.
- Repent of apathy or luke-warmness when entering His presence.

DAY 9: LIVING PURE
IN AN UNCLEAN WORLD

"So I tell you this, and insist on it in the Lord, that you must no longer live as the (world*) Gentiles do, in the futility of their thinking. They are darkened in their understanding and separated from the life of God. . . ."
(Ephesians 4:17-18) *added for emphasis

There is a desire in all of us to be normal in the world in which we are born. God is not interested in us being normal, but supernatural! The world places their identity and stability in outward things. They focus on what they can have, hold or see. The world says this is normal. But, God did not call us to be normal. God wants to flood our lives with the same power that raised Christ Jesus from the dead!

Living pure in an unclean world means we are not seeking God for things (Matthew 6:33). We are not looking for satisfaction or fulfillment through fleshly pursuits or pleasures. Especially when we get stressed, we often turn to social media, entertainment, food and addictions of various kinds to ease the tension. This is where idolatry starts. A heart pursuing holiness will look first to God. Idols will strip us of our focus, finances, security and significance from being rooted in Christ. Psalm 119:9-11 says, "How can a young man keep his way pure? By living according to your word." It is only through staying true to His Word that we can have clean hands and a pure heart.

PERSONAL ACTION POINTS
*   Are you daily hiding God's Word in your heart to keep your way pure?
*   Can you identify any "idols of distraction" in your life or unhealthy ways of dealing with stress?
*   Ask for a cleansing of these idols and for a pure passion for Him.

CORPORATE ACTION POINTS
*   Repent of ways in which the Church isn't demonstrating purity in actions or words.
*   Ask the Holy Spirit to increase our passion for His presence when tempted to fill our lives with activities or programs that He hasn't ordained.
*   Pray for grace to be in the world but not of it.

DAY 10: THE SAFEST PLACE TO BE

"If you make the Most High your dwelling, even the LORD, who is my refuge, then no harm will befall you, no disaster will come near your tent"
(Psalm 91:9-10).

We don't usually associate holiness with protection, but Psalm 91 lists a whole host of promises that come to those who dwell in His presence. He is a holy God; therefore, His presence is Holy. When we learn to abide in this place of His holiness He tells us that no harm will come near us. He will cover us with His wings, just like the cherubim above the Ark of the Covenant, because He is a covenant God.

But what about all the times when harm does come? What about when disaster does strike? The verse does suggest a prerequisite before the promises. We must make His presence our dwelling. That means not just a visit once in a while. That means we must learn to make this a daily habit of living. We must practice His presence and not just visit with Him once or twice a week.

Luke 1:74-75 states that we can "serve him without fear in holiness and righteousness." There is a correlation to living in holiness and being free from fear. When we truly live from that place of being sheltered, covered and overshadowed by the Most High God, we are in the safest place possible. He is the One who is in charge and will take care of our enemies. These are the promises that are ours as we daily draw close to His presence and His holiness.

PERSONAL ACTION POINTS
- Do you fear harm or destruction?
- Confess fears.
- Consider ways to draw closer to His holiness and live in His presence.
- Read the entire Psalm 91 as your personal promise.

CORPORATE ACTION POINTS
- Repent of any tendency to avoid His holiness out of fear or unbelief. Pray for deliverance from fears of every kind.
- Ask the Holy Spirit to renew minds to embrace His holiness as a place of safety and adoration.

DAY 11: FACE TIME WITH GOD

"Hear, O LORD, when I cry with my voice! Have mercy also upon me, and answer me. When You said, "Seek My face," my heart said to You, "Your face, LORD, I will seek" (Psalms 27:7-8 NKJV).

Face time creates true friendships! Three people are named in the Bible as being friends of God: Abraham (James 2:23), Moses (Exodus 33:11), and us! (John 15:15).

What qualifies a friendship with God? For Abraham, it was taking God at His word before he saw the evidence of God's promise. For Moses, it was setting aside uninterrupted time outside of his routine to get into His presence. For us, it's when we learn to know His heart beyond our service for Him.

In Numbers 12:6-8, God states how he speaks to His people. Through prophets he uses dreams and visions, but "with him (Moses) I speak face to face, clearly and not in riddles." Face time with God brings us into real time! When we set aside time to hear clearly from him, his holiness floods us. Holiness is not a rule book we follow but a room we enter with the person of God! (Hebrews 4:15-16).

Having face time with God can be unnerving to our flesh. Sitting before God with no agenda but to listen is awkward for some. Yet, those who have broken the barrier of sitting in silence have found deliverance of sins that have plagued them for years. They have seen breakthrough in families with loved ones saved and a deepened connection with God.

PERSONAL ACTION POINTS
- What is standing in the way of developing your friendship with God?
- If you feel a "disconnect" or "static" with God, ask Him to show you what's hindering your friendship with Him.
- Sit in silence and listen for God to speak.

CORPORATE ACTION POINTS
- Do you make time for Face Time with God as a family, small group or ministry?
- Ask the Holy Spirit to reveal ways in which to enter this holy place corporately in order to deepen friendship with God.

DAY 12: POLITICALLY CORRECT OR BIBLICALLY TRUE?

"Obey God because you are his children. Don't slip back into your old ways of doing evil; you didn't know any better then. But now you must be holy in everything you do, just as God—who chose you to be his children—is holy" (1 Peter 1:13-15 NLT).

"In everything you do," is literally translated as "all manner of conversation." Our behaviors and conversations change when Christ has entered our hearts! That's living holiness when even our speech is set apart.

Jesus used salt to illustrate our distinctiveness when He stated that we are the "salt of the earth." He said if we lose our saltiness, we are essentially worthless and have no distinction from the world (Matthew 5:13).

In our culture today, evil is emphasized more than good. Political pressure is rising to call good evil and evil good. Do we know the difference? 2 Timothy 3:16 reads: "All Scripture is given by inspiration of God, and is profitable for doctrine, for reproof, for correction and for instruction in righteousness."

True holiness establishes firm biblical convictions based on Scriptural principles, not personal preferences. Political correctness calls for compromise. We have a daily choice as to how we talk about Christ and our relationship with Him. The world will always pressure us to cave in. In the end, we must obey God rather than men! (Acts 5:29).

PERSONAL ACTION POINTS
- Do you find yourself giving in to keep the peace or to be liked?
- Repent of any compromise you have made in your speech or conduct.
- Ask for God's standard in your life to remain secure.

CORPORATE ACTION POINTS
- Confess any ways in which the Church has compromised biblical standards for social acceptance.
- Repent for not having a deeper conviction of God's heart and ways.
- Ask the Holy Spirit to bring greater revelation of His Word and a passion to stand firm in Truth.

DAY 13: HOLY AND HAPPY

"There is a river whose streams make glad the city of God,
the holy place where the Most High dwells.
God is within her, she will not fall" (Psalm 46:4-5).

In defining Holiness as being "set apart" versus being "religious," we are now positioned to realize the joy of this amazing relationship. Although our flesh may cringe in the presence of a Holy God, our spirits rejoice! The closer we draw to His throne of grace, the greater is His desire to remove any roadblocks to His presence. This brings Him great joy and we, too, can experience this joy.

Jesus was a happy person. He didn't go to sinners as much as they went to Him. Here was the holiest person ever to live and yet the worst of sinners were drawn to Him. Though He literally carried the world on His shoulders, He "rejoiced" (Luke 10:21), was ""full of joy" (John 15:11) and had a "full measure of joy" (John 17:13). He enjoyed His relationship with His Father and it showed. People wanted to be near Him.

We have bought the lie that if we are to reach sinners, we need to be like them; when in fact, Jesus was the exact opposite. His sole desire was to be just like His Father. He wouldn't do or say anything that His Father did not initiate! He demonstrated the ability to be holy and happy at the same time!

PERSONAL ACTION POINTS
• Have you equated holiness with seriousness?
• Have you compromised His holiness hoping to attract unbelievers?
• Confess these ungodly mindsets and ask the Lord to renew your mind and heart.

CORPORATE ACTION POINTS
• Repent of attitudes or actions that have brought a yoke of oppression instead of joy.
• Ask the Lord to free us from any religious mindset that says we can't be holy and happy at the same time.
• Ask the Lord to draw sinners to Christ as a result of our joy and praise.

DAY 14: NO HOLINESS, NO PRESENCE

"Make every effort to live in peace with all men and to be holy; without holiness no one will see the Lord" (Hebrews 12:14).

There is a troubling tendency in the Body of Christ today to believe that if we just have enough passion and prayer, we will experience the fullness of God's manifest presence. Though there may be isolated testimonies of such occurrences, they usually don't last over the long-haul. Scripture is clear that if we want to see God, we must be holy.

Previous spiritual awakenings have taught us that if we are not walking in purity of heart, integrity and right relationships, we will not be able to maintain His presence, no matter how powerful or anointed it seems. This is true at every level, starting at home and in our congregations. As we pursue more of His presence, we must also pursue holiness.

God doesn't just want to come for a short while; He wants to stay. That requires a holy people who can steward His presence and all that He wants to pour out. It will require people who have proven themselves faithful to His Word and heart and are ready to carry His presence with humility, grace and wisdom.

Passion and vision may be the initiators of this journey to transformation, but it's living a holy life that will ultimately determine whether or not we can rightly steward a supernatural outpouring.

PERSONAL ACTION POINTS
- Are you committed to embracing holiness as a lifestyle, not just a doctrine?
- Confess any tendency to want a quick fix rather than pursue a daily walk of integrity, purity and right relationships.

CORPORATE ACTION POINTS
- Does our corporate worship reflect holiness as much as zeal and passion?
- Confess ways in which we have tried to take shortcuts to spiritual awakening. Repent of any belief system which has placed temporary spiritual experiences above a life of daily devotion.

WEEK THREE
UNITY versus DIVISION

DAY 15: UNITY DEFINED

*"Whatever happens, conduct yourselves in a manner worthy of the gospel
of Christ. Then, ... I will know that you stand firm in one spirit,
contending as one man for the faith of the gospel without being frightened
in any way by those who oppose you" (Philippians 1:27-28).*

Unity defined is "the state of being united or joined as a whole." Jesus defines unity as "oneness" with Him and the Father through the bond of the Holy Spirit. "I pray also for those who will believe in me through their message, that all of them may be one, Father, just as you are in me and I am in you" (John 17:20). The Father, Son and Holy Spirit are the perfect picture of Unity. We don't create unity, but we are told to keep it (Ephesians 4:3) as a reflection of the Father's divine nature.

Unity is a powerful force for good or for evil. Division is usually the result of living in disobedience to the Word of God. Jesus did not pray for us to do great miracles or to bring people into his Kingdom. He specifically prayed for his Body to be in unity, which would automatically result in evangelism! "May they also be in us so that the world may believe that you have sent me" (John 17:21).

What will it require of us as His church in this city to fulfill this request? Our unity will come as a result of our connection to the Head. "They will be my people, and I will be their God. I will give them singleness of heart and action, so that they will always fear me for their own good and the good of their children after them" (Jeremiah 32:38-39).

PERSONAL ACTION POINTS

- Confess any ways in which you have been divisive by placing issues above relationships.
- Repent of any self-defense tendencies.
- Ask the Lord for singleness of heart and action in order to be an agent of unity.

CORPORATE ACTION POINTS

- Confess any ways in which unity has been undermined in the Church by people focusing on "right or wrong" instead of healthy relationships.
- Ask for greater capacity to love others for the sake of the Kingdom.

DAY 16: THE HIGH CALL OF HONOR

"Be devoted to one another in brotherly love. Honor one another above yourselves" (Romans 12:9-10).

Danny Silk, author of *A Culture of Honor,* describes honor as "the relational tool that protects the value that people have for those who are different than they are." It's easy to honor and value someone who thinks like you do. But, when you are in a family (biological or spiritual) with differing ideals and values, it's more of a challenge. This is when we must demonstrate brotherly love and truly honor one another.

We must separate the things that are dogma (the uncompromising essentials of the gospel), doctrine (various interpretations of faith practices like baptisms, eschatology, spiritual gifts, etc.) and opinion (personal preferences). While we should all agree on dogma regarding our salvation and the person of Jesus, there will always be differences in various doctrines and even more differences of opinion! In these latter two areas, we must operate in much grace towards one another and honor the journeys we are each on.

Honoring one another is looking beyond someone's belief system and recognizing them as God does—someone who needs the same grace you do—and honoring their God-given gifts and place in the body. God is not obligating us to agree on everything, but to rise above our differences and love as Christ does. This will be the true test of our love for Him. In honoring each other, we honor Him.

PERSONAL ACTION POINTS
- Have you personally settled your own dogma, doctrine and opinion? Repent of any ways in which you have put pressure on others to agree with your opinions.
- Seek forgiveness if needed.

CORPORATE ACTION POINTS
- Ask the Holy Spirit to show areas where you have made your opinion or doctrinal issues, dogmatic or divisive within the Body. Ask for forgiveness.
- Ask the Lord how you can demonstrate honor towards others and affirm the work of God in the lives of those around you.

Day 17: The Value of Each One

"But God has put the body together, giving greater honor to the parts that lacked it, so that there should be no division in the body, but that its parts should have equal concern for each other" (1 Corinthians 12:24-25).

It's hard to argue with someone you really care about. When you truly value someone, you treat the differences with care. God has specifically put people together for a purpose. To fulfill God's call, we must value each other and our unique contributions, both at home and in the church.

Not everyone operates as the mouth and not everyone has the grace to be the foot. But, each part has been graced by God to be an integral part of the whole. If we walk in humility together, we will see one another's gifts and contributions as part of something much bigger. No one can fulfill the call of God on their own. We need one another in order to be all that we were created to be. We can't receive the fullness of God's favor and blessing until we all reach unity and work as one (Ephesians 4:13).

Jealousy has no room in this kind of atmosphere. If we are jealous of another's gift, we have been blinded to the unique part that we play and are missing our blessing. We are also telling God that we don't like the part He gave us and we are robbing the other person of the blessing God intends for them. When we see each other as God does, we will begin to value each other and rejoice in the role that each plays.

Personal Action Points
- Have you been jealous of another person's gift?
- Repent and ask God to change your heart towards them.
- Has God been trying to reach you through someone else's gift? Receive it and bless it!

Corporate Action Points
- Repent of ways in which you have been jealous of other people and of the way God is using them.
- Verbally thank those whom the Lord is using to bless the body.
- Instead of focusing on your own puzzle piece, ask God how we all fit together in His church in this community.

DAY 18: TO WHOM ARE WE BOUND?

*"They will ask the way to Zion and turn their faces toward it.
They will come and bind themselves to the LORD in an everlasting
covenant that will not be forgotten (Jeremiah 50:5).*

God is a covenant God. He keeps His promises and He is zealous for those who have bound themselves to His heart. He makes covenant with us as a way to show that He is totally committed to us, and will remain faithful in His dealings with us. Our part is to keep this covenant by not letting anyone or anything get in between us and our first love.

Unfortunately, we face many opportunities to allow other people and other priorities access to that place in our hearts that should be reserved solely for Him. This becomes evident whenever someone or something else trumps God's will for our lives. When we begin to please other people, even family members, over and above God, we are not keeping our covenant. Sometimes, there are ungodly soul ties that are in place which keep us bound to someone else that must be broken in order to restore our relationship with God. Sometimes, we can get bound up in our jobs or businesses in an unhealthy way. Or, to fraternities or civic organizations where we make unnecessary oaths or vows that spiritually bind us and break our covenant with God.

We must be alert to our heart condition. If God is not first in our focus and priorities, we cannot walk in the fullness of His covenant with us.

PERSONAL ACTION POINTS
- Is there someone or something in your life that is pulling on your heart stronger than the Lord?
- Confess this and break any ungodly soul ties binding up your heart.
- Renew your covenant with the Lord and your desire to put Him first.

CORPORATE ACTION POINTS
- Are we unified in our covenant with the Lord in our homes and churches?
- Do we seek His heart above all else and everyone else?
- Repent of any way in which you have allowed your own preferences or priorities to stand in the way of healthy covenant in the Body of Christ.

DAY 19: LIVING UNOFFENDABLE

"He who covers over an offense promotes love, but whoever repeats the matter separates close friends" (Proverbs 17:9 NIV).

One of the greatest obstacles to community transformation is carrying internal offenses. James 4:1-4 describes quarrels and fights as a product of self-centered thinking. Jesus, full of heaven's power, was limited in healings and miracles in his own home town because the people were offended at him (Mark 6:3-6). Solomon writes in Proverbs 18:19 that it's easier to capture a barricaded city than to reason with an offended person.

Taking an offense is a matter of our choice. It's not put upon us. However, we can live unoffendable lives just as Jesus did. 1 Peter 2:23 states: "When they hurled their insults at him, he did not retaliate; when he suffered, he made no threats. Instead, he entrusted himself to him who judges justly."

Offenses come to us in three categories:
- Direct (from one to another)
- Indirect (someone else's offense we hear about second-hand)
- Corporate (everyone in the whole organization or church "did me wrong")

The way out is forgiveness! Forgive the person and what they did to offend you. Holding onto the offense only keeps you in bondage (John 20:23). When you forgive, you get free from the offense and you walk lighter, think clearer, and are empowered to be victorious in other areas. Determine to not get trapped by offense and live unoffendable.

PERSONAL ACTION POINTS
- Is there someone who has offended you?
- Choose to forgive and seek out reconciliation, not pursue who is "right."
- If you have taken an indirect offense, forgive and release the situation to the Lord.

CORPORATE ACTION POINTS
- Repent of any ways bitterness has taken root because of past offenses.
- Ask the Lord for a new heart and new perspective to start building and strengthening relationships at home and in the church.
- Pray grace on leaders who deal with conflicts on a regular basis.

DAY 20: THE CALL FOR CRITICAL CARE

"If one part suffers, every part suffers with it; if one part is honored,
every part rejoices with it" (1 Corinthians 12:26).

As we journey towards a transformed heart where God's love rules over every relationship and priority, we will begin to have God's heartbeat for others. Once we are secure in our relationship with the Lord and settled in our identity, we are free to care for each other without any strings attached. This is when "agape" love is felt and displayed, when it is given freely and generously.

Notice also that the Scripture says if one part is honored, every part will rejoice. This means that when someone else is commended, recognized and affirmed, we will not only welcome it, but rejoice in it! In like manner, when one part is hurting, every part will be affected by the pain and suffering. This is what God has always intended for the family of God—to complete one another. As we learn to live from His heart, the many will become one and each part will serve the other.

Today, there are many hurting people around us. People are in need of critical care. Over and above practical helps, people need a big dose of unconditional love and acceptance. Our call as believers is to provide the intensive "TLC" (tender, loving care) needed. We can only do this when our own needs are no longer an issue. There is a growing call for critical care to be the agents of an amazing outpouring of God's love and grace.

PERSONAL ACTION POINTS

- Do you have a sensitive heart towards the needs of others or are you too preoccupied with your own?
- Ask the Lord for a download of His grace and love towards others needs.
- Ask God who needs critical care around you and become an answer to that person's prayers.

CORPORATE ACTION POINTS

- Are we caring for orphans and widows as Scripture instructs (James 1:27)?
- Repent of self-preoccupation or apathy towards the needy.
- Ask the Lord for any needed heart change towards those needs and the practical helps to meet them.

DAY 21: YOU MUST BE PRESENT TO WIN!

"In him the whole building is joined together and rises to become a holy temple in the Lord. And in him you too are being built together to become a dwelling in which God lives by his Spirit" (Ephesians 2:21-22).

If you've ever put your name in a drawing for a prize, many times there's the rule "Must be Present to Win." Unless you show up in person, you're not qualified to get the prize.

As believers we are told to run in such a way as to get the prize (1 Corinthians 9:24). This prize is our reward for being faithful to the call on our lives and finishing everything we were given to do. This instruction is not only for individuals but also for the Body of Christ. We have been given a mandate, a charge, a race that we've been called to win. Just like a relay race, everyone has a strategic part. But, if you're not present, it will affect everyone else and thus, the whole team may be disqualified.

Our culture is not too keen on teamwork. Individualism is esteemed and touted as the ultimate demonstration of strength, ability and success. In the kingdom, however, it's just the opposite. We are at our best when everyone works together. Paul wrote that the Body is, "… joined and held together by every supporting ligament, (and) grows and builds itself up in love, as each part does its work" (Ephesians 4:16).

If we want to win the race to see our communities transformed by the manifest presence of God, we need to be present. That means engaged through our prayers, priorities and practices. Corporate worship and intercession is a primary key in demonstrating our unity and positioning our hearts in humility and holiness. God is looking for a place for His presence to rest. We are living stones being built into a place for His glory to dwell. May we embrace and enjoy the journey together!

"Let us go to his dwelling place; let us worship at his footstool. Arise, O LORD, and come to your resting place, you and the ark of your might. May your priests be clothed with righteousness; may your saints sing for joy" (Psalm 132:7-9).

ABOUT THE AUTHORS

Bobby Alger is Lead Pastor at Crossroads Community Church in Winchester, Virginia which he and Wanda planted in 1998. He has led numerous prayer retreats for pastors and community prayer initiatives in their city. He also provides apostolic oversight to several leaders and fellowships within their region.

Wanda Alger is a prophetic teacher, intercessor, and the author of several books including "Moving from Sword to Scepter: Ruling Through Prayer as the Ekklesia of God." She has been a field correspondent with Intercessors for America and has published articles with Charisma, The Elijah List, and The Christian Post.

Church website: crossroadswinchester.com

Wanda's website: wandaalger.me

NOTES

NOTES

NOTES

Made in the USA
Coppell, TX
28 January 2023

11852546R00023